Eventually, all our desires will synthesize to one —to embody happiness in the eternal now.

Copyright © 2015 by Marilu Garbi.
Pictures in the cover and interior of the book by © Marilu Garbi.

This book is not a prescription for happiness. There is no formula for that. It's instead the result of a continuous self reflecting process that has made me realize that happiness is our default, and that the only reason we don't experience this natural state, is because of the beliefs that we have adopted as absolute unmalleable truths.

Therefore, you assume full responsibility for your reception and use of—and results from—this book, and for your own well being. You understand that any reproduction or distribution of the material in this book to third parties without the express written consent of Marilu Garbi is prohibited.

ISBN 978-0-9963640-0-3

Shakti Coil Publishing

@marilugarbi

Table of Content

Introduction	5
Thank You	6
What's in the Way of Your Happiness?	7
How do you change undeserving beliefs?	14
Are your emotions overwhelming, making it impossible to find a reason to be grateful?	24
How can you make your ego an ally in creation?	32
What if your desires are harmful to others?	38
But what if others judge you?	42
What if you feel abused by others?	46
Why do your lvoved ones bother you the most?	50
About the author	55
Appendix: Invitation to Self-Reflect	57

*We didn't come here to learn any lessons, but to release fears.
That's our contribution to life's evolution*

Introduction

This book was born from the pages of my journal during one of the most difficult times in my life—when I separated from the father of my kids. I made a lot of mistakes in an attempt to seek balance and fulfillment, trying to cure an incessant—yet subtle—feeling of being trapped. I couldn't reconcile responsibility with fun; caring for others with caring for myself; self-expression with duty; so I ran away from it all. On my journey back and forth from home, I gained the wisdom I share in this book. Each word intends to awaken your self-reflection, which will ultimately lead you to the realization that happiness is your default—your natural state of being.

Thank You

To all who have shared an instant in space and time with me. Thank you for inspiring me and making me crazy at times. I now know that, no matter how sweet or sour our relationship has been, we are all guided by a single intention–to get better and offer the best of us to the world.

What's in the way of your happiness?

Taking all your thoughts seriously.

Happiness is not something that you can pursue, learn, take, or even wish for; it's simply what's left after you replace beliefs that don't serve you any longer.

You take your thoughts seriously because you believe that they are true. There's so much evidence in your past that supports this [relative] truth that it seems unfathomable to believe that there are other [relative] truths. But one day, after suffering enough, you realize that this truth was just a belief and you have the power to replace it for a new one that supports your expansion, your unique and joyful expression.

Beliefs aren't harmful. They give us a reason to create (if I hadn't believed that I was a writer, I couldn't have produced this book, for example). What hurts is to think that they are absolute-fixed-truths. Beliefs are like shoes—meant to be changed as we grow and as seasons require.

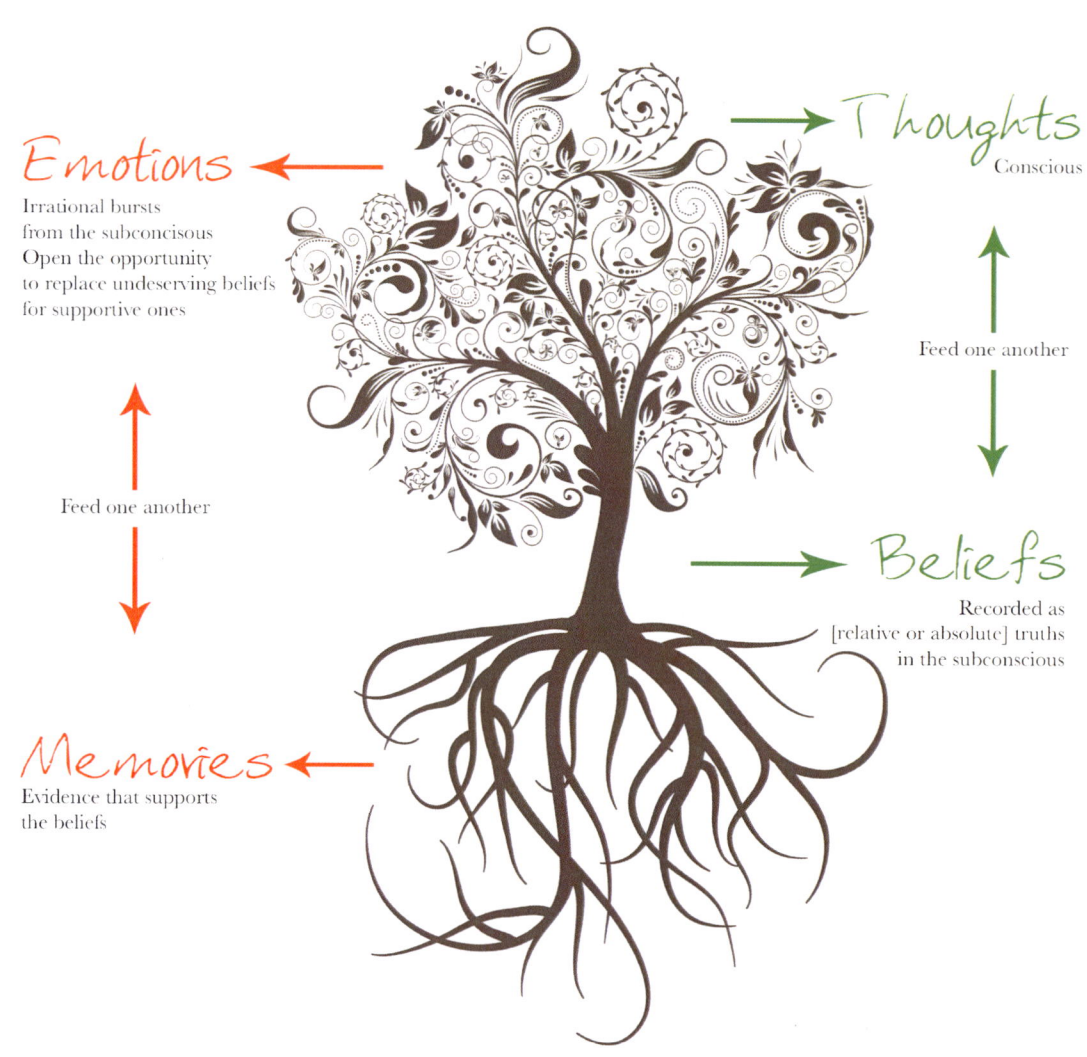

No belief holds any [absolute] truth.

When you are bothered by a situation—your kids leaving their clean clothes on the floor, for example —there is an undeserving belief behind it, supporting it from your subconscious. Your messy room must have upset your mom, which made you believe that you were causing her discomfort because the "truth was that you were doing something wrong and she had the right to be upset." Since truths cannot be changed, you doomed yourself to repeat your mom's behavior and to being bothered by disorderly rooms. After all, you wanted to be right, just like your mom was.

The good news is that beliefs have a switch called truth. You can turn them off—and stop their influence over your life—by believing that they are just a story which can never hold any absolute truth.

How do you change undeserving beliefs?

By living (being bothered) and self-reflecting, living (being bothered again) and self-reflecting...

Only when you have suffered enough for holding undeserving beliefs as truthful do you have the power to change them.

But only after you allow yourself to feel the emotions linked to those beliefs do you gain the power to replace or let them go.

The bottom line is that you'll keep facing circumstances that you dislike until you can find a reason to be grateful for them; not by changing the circumstances, but by first changing your perception. This is what unconditional love really means—to love your life no matter what the circumstances are.

Willingly or not, your actions are leading you to a place of less resistance, where your likes and dislikes matter less. You'll understand that gratitude for all that happens in your life is the only doorway to embody happiness in the eternal now—the only life's purpose there is.

Keep shifting your perspective until the door of gratitude opens. Don't ever give up. I assure you that there's always a reason to be grateful, no matter how traumatic the circumstance is.

Are your emotions overwhelming, making it impossible to find a reason to be grateful?

AOL
Allow, observe, let go.

Emotions are bundles of energy trapped in your body. They just want your attention and validation. Like kids, they won't stop crying until you acknowledge them. Allow yourself to vent in private or in the company of a good listener. Observe your unedited—and at times disturbing—thoughts by getting them out of your head into a voice recorder. Let Go of them by listening to the recording as many times as necessary until you start smiling.

Your life is a story that you happen to believe is true.

As creator, you are given the power of meaning; not by purposely assigning it, but by reflecting your beliefs into the World.

The beliefs that we have been talking about are made out of thoughts that construct a narrative, the story of you or more accurately of your personality, your ego.
Enlightened beings have reported this information to humanity before, advising us to focus our attention on the true self, the unchangeable, the ethereal and eternal. But the world where we live now —where ego is indispensable to our [social] survival—forces us to work with our ego, educate it instead of subduing it, exploit it instead of fighting it, love it instead of fearing it.

How can you make your ego an ally in creation?

By educating it.

The ego is nothing more than an instrument for creation, the engine that propels your unique action into the world. But it must ride in the passenger seat of your life. As a driver, it creates a troublesome world in which you live to take without considering the impact on the whole.

You must educate your ego by understanding that:

A. You are an inseparable part of the universe—a holographic particle of it.

B. Your actions—consciously or not—impact the whole.

C. You can only enjoy your life as creator when you let go of the expectation of a specific outcome. From this educated ego only mindful action can emerge making corrective/punishing systems, such as government and religion, obsolete.

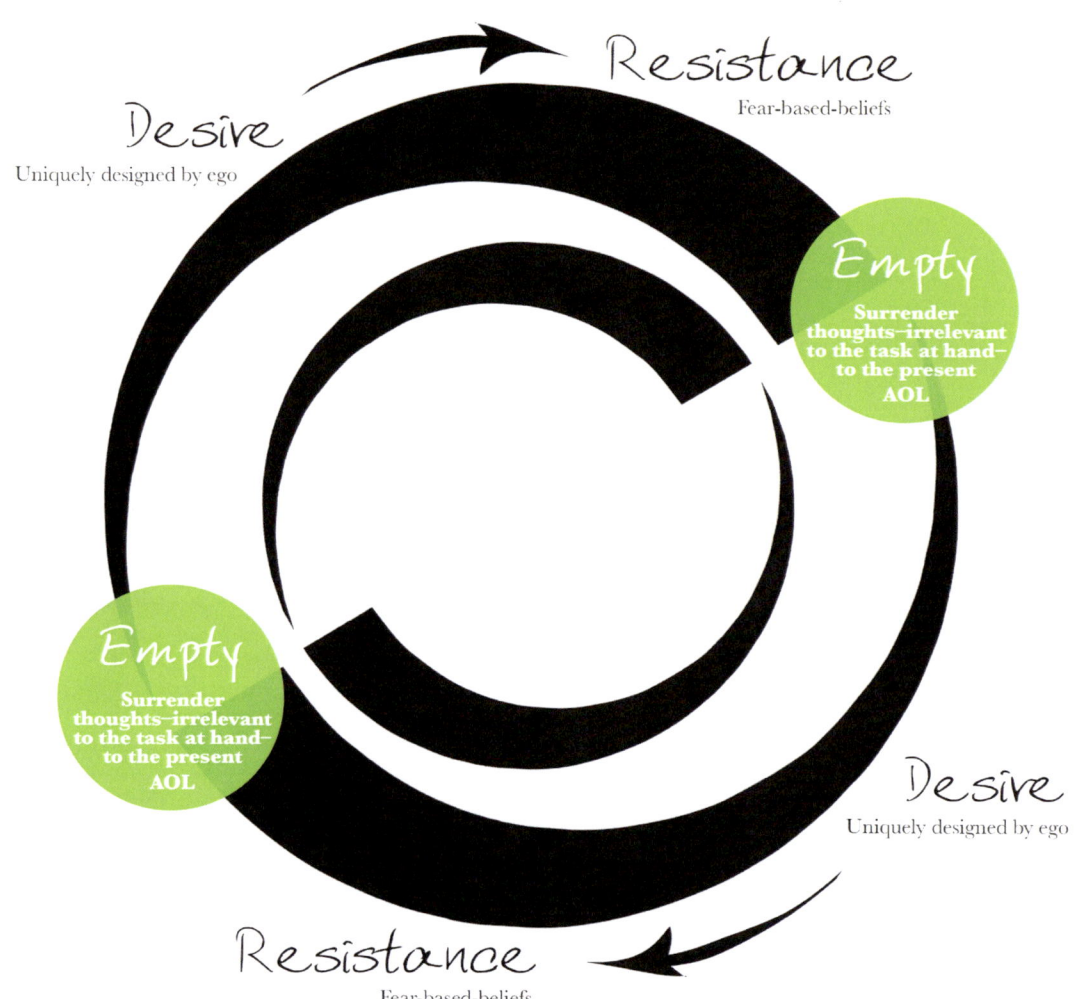

At the root of every dissatisfaction is a belief that is stopping you from realizing your desires. Only by acting on your unique desires, without expecting a specific result, can you fulfill your life's purpose—to embody happiness in the eternal now.

As a creator, you'll inevitably desire. In the pursuit of desires, you'll meet your resistances—fear- based beliefs—so you can release them.

Every desire is paired with the resistance that you are ready to let go in that moment. When you avoid this pursuit—because you believe it is bad—you only increase your frustration and your desire for more, combined with guilt and the need for self-punishment. You find yourself in a tug of war where you're pulled by "I should be in one direction," and by "I want to be in the opposite."

Have you tried to appease the craving for a chocolate cake with a healthy granola bar? It simply doesn't work. You usually end up ingesting more calories with various substitutes and feeling guilty on top of it. The very act of labeling the desire as bad is what attracts you to it.

What if you're kind to yourself instead and have that chocolate cake. You'll be surprise at how little you need to fulfill your desire if you stop suppressing it.

What if your desires are harmful to others?

You're always doing your best to get better and you can't harm others without their permission.

You compromise your happiness to be responsible to others when all others need from you is your happiness.

Your desires are guided by a deeper and universal intention that wants the best for you, that wants you to unburden fears and to accept you as you actually are; with flaws, mistakes and all. Understanding that even the most despicable crimes have been perpetuated with this intention allows you to forgive and frees you from resentment, regret and revenge.

This doesn't mean that you won't make corrections when realizing an error in your behavior. It only means that it's okay to make mistakes because they shape you into a humbler and wiser human being.

But what if others judge you?

Judgement is nothing more than self-opinion.

We judge when we don't know ourselves well enough.

Either when the judgment is coming from you or from others [who are really a projection of an aspect of you], it can only affect you if you believe it's true. Easier to say than to do because in the moment, emotions are triggered and you lose perspective of reality. As much as you can, remember that all perspectives are valid. Everyone is right in his/her own perception. We all have good reasons to judge, so don't fight it. Don't take it personally or seriously and especially avoid taking a position. What are you defending anyway?

What if you feel abused by others?

Give them your honest feedback.

Loving others doesn't mean putting up with them, but offering them your most honest feedback.

This human experience is more about learning to deal with unconsciousness than consciousness because the truth is that we are all constantly evolving, transforming and learning. You may have transcended your resistance against money, but your spouse hasn't. Are you going to stop loving him/her? You can't. The love that bounds you to different relationships forces you to deal with what bothers you in others. AOL can be used for that.

But you also need to express to the other person in the relationship—as emotionless and clearly as possible—your dislikes. You need to offer your honest feedback when something bothers you, no matter how irrational your reasons are. For example, you hate that your husband snores. Instead of putting up with it and accumulating resentment, tell him. Be honest with yourself and give your feedback the next morning. What he does next doesn't really matter, because you already benefited by releasing the harmful thought and feeling.

Why do your loved ones bother you the most?

Because they serve as mirrors of the aspects of yourself that are most difficult for you to accept.

All relationships are divinely designed to assist you in transcending an aspect of yourself.

Remember that you are an inseparable part of the whole and that you can't harm others without their permission. Relationships are the manifestations of this principle. In practical terms, you are responsible for co-creating the reality that you share. You will feel attracted to people—and have a desire to engage in a relationship with them—because they complement you. If you're a control freak, you'll be attracted to people that want to be controlled. But also, if you are denying an aspect of yourself, you'll spot it in another and be bothered by it. That's why it's said that we all serve as mirrors for one another.

I am an ordinary woman. I thought that my life's purpose was to inspire women to find, nurture and speak clearly their intuitive and wise voices. Then I realized that by focusing on helping others I was missing the point. The only reason I'm alive is to outrageously be me, fearless and joyful.

In order to embody this realization, I had to muster the courage to live beyond my culture and history, free from the past and innocent into the future. I finally understood that inspiring others was a side effect of simply living an authentic life.

Marilu Garbi is a certified Scrum Master and the founder of Well Formed Teams, a consulting firm that assists small and medium-size companies in the implementation of agile principles to improve their work environments, increase productivity, and bring more value to their customers. She has 20 years of experience as a business owner of a print shop in Naples FL. She holds a bachelor's degree in journalism from the Universidad Central de Venezuela and an Associate of Applied Science degree in film and TV production. She spent four years writing for a Venezuelan news radio station and a year as a reporter for a local TV channel before moving to the United States in 2000 to start a family.

Marilu's writing includes the scripts for two short films, Thinking Out Loud (2018) and In Tango (2019), which she also produced and performed in.

Marilu has been published in the Elephant Journal, Inspire Me Today, and writes for her personal blog, Downloads of Wisdom. She also hosted the radio program Meaningful Connections on BlogTalkRadio.

In her spare time she does Improv Theatre and dances the Argentinian tango with her life partner.

You can follow her on Facebook and Instagram @marilugarbi

Appendix

Invitation to Self-Reflect

Every month, randomly pick one of the following pages, cut it out and tape it on your bathroom mirror or any other visible area of your house. Journal your insights.

Believes are like shoes: You get new ones when you grow and change the style to adapt to the season.

Marilu Garbi

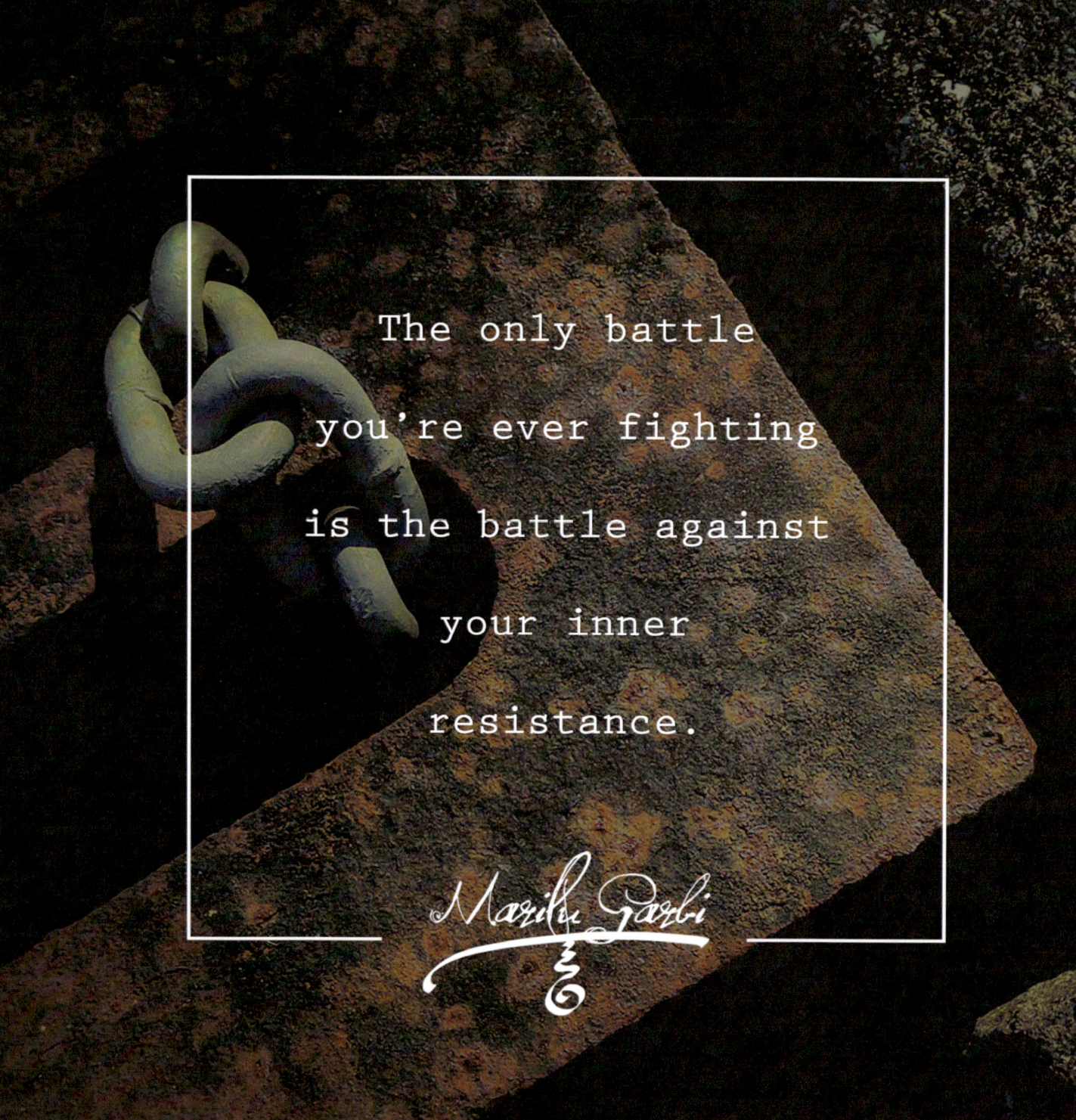

> There's no purpose to life beyond the enjoyment of the moment. We all came here to play.
>
> — Marilu Garbi

> What's required to live the life of your dreams is less effort and more focus on what makes your heart sing.
>
> — *Marilu Garbi*

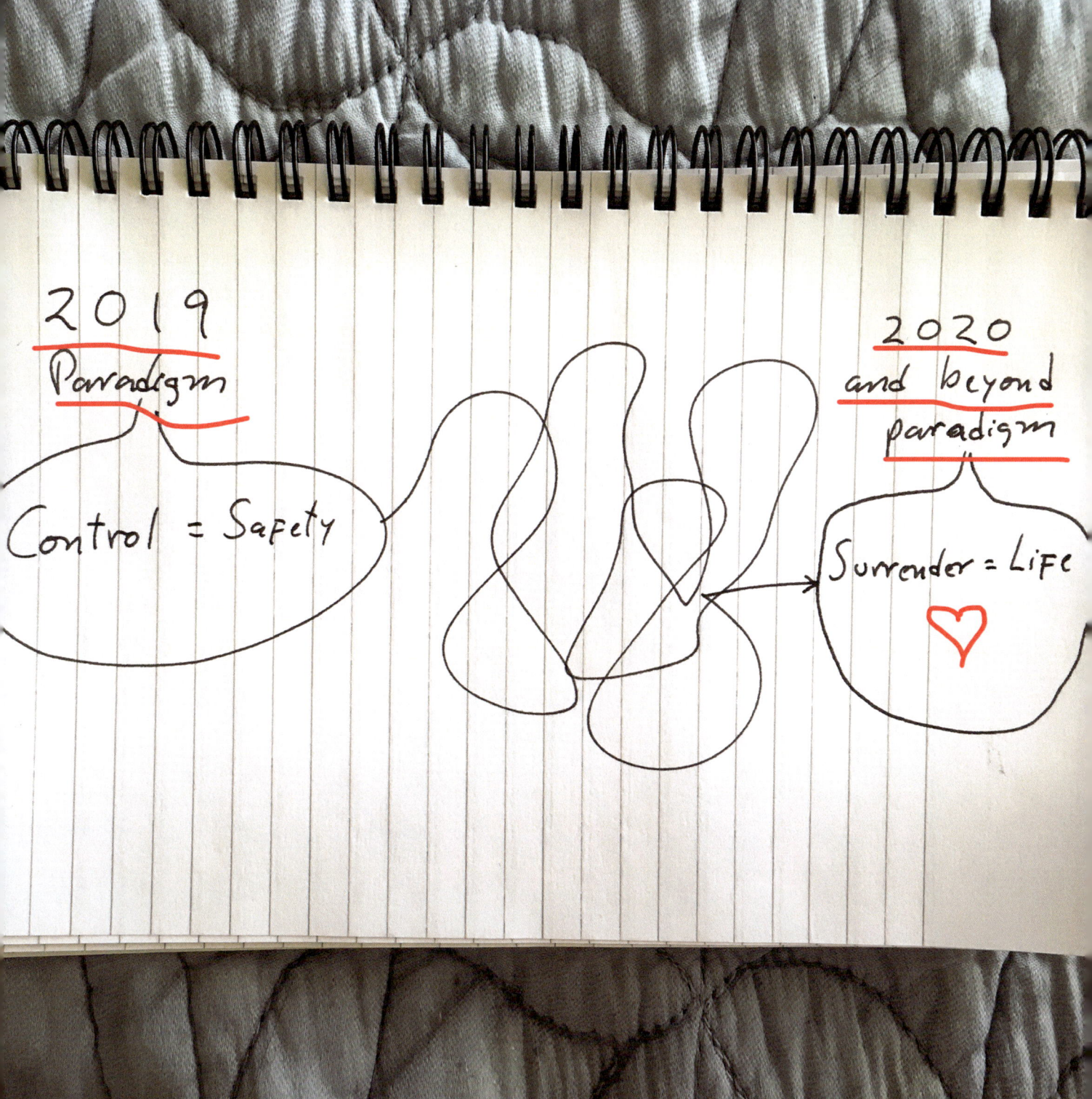

www.ingramcontent.com/pod-product-compliance
Lightning Source LLC
Chambersburg PA
CBRC092342290426
44110CB00008B/183